The Lord's Prayer

The Lord's Prayer

A *commentary by*

ST. CYPRIAN
OF CARTHAGE

Translated for meditation by
EDMOND BONIN

Christian Classics
P. O. Box 30
Westminster, MD 21157

1983

First Published in English, 1983

ISBN: 0-87061-076-7
Library of Congress Catalog Card Number: 83-71388
Copyright © 1983 by Christian Classics, Inc.
All Rights Reserved
Printed in United States of America

Contents

Part III: Further thoughts on prayer   83

Translator's foreword

Biographical sketch of St. Cyprian

Caecilius Cyprianus Thascius was born between 200 and 210 A.D., most probably in Carthage, North Africa. The son of a rich and highly cultured pagan family, he studied rhetoric and soon became famous as a lawyer and master of eloquence. Though worldly and dissipated—"a stranger to the truth and the light," as he says in his *Ad Donatum*—he grew increasingly disgusted with immorality in both public and private life as well as with corruption in government. At this point, an old priest by the name of Caecilius gave him a Bible, and grace did the rest.

It was a difficult decision for Cyprian; but once he had made it, there were no regrets, no half measures. When he embraced Christianity in 245, he abandoned his lucrative law practice and distributed his fortune among the poor; he likewise renounced pagan literature and devoted himself exclusively to reading Scripture and Tertullian. Shortly afterwards, he was ordained a priest and, in 248 or early 249, was consecrated bishop of Carthage "by the will of God and the voice of the people."[1]

In 250, the Emperor Decius launched a persecution which, for the first time, affected all Roman subjects: everyone, throughout the Empire, was to offer sacrifice. Cyprian went into hiding for some fourteen months, "not so much for my own safety," he explained to his critics, "as for the public peace of the Church, lest my presence provoke further disturbance."[2] The twenty-seven letters we have from this period testify that he kept in touch with his clergy and his flock. As he himself put it, he may

---

[1] *Vita Cypriani*, purportedly written by Pontius, his deacon.
[2] *Letter 20.*

have been "absent in body, but not in spirit or deed or counsel."

Upon his return to Carthage in the spring of 251, he had to deal with a problem that had developed in his absence: what to do about the *lapsi,* those who had denied their faith during the persecution and now wanted to be reconciled with the Church. Some of the clergy and laity demanded immediate reconciliation for all, while bishop and synod insisted on a period of penance proportionate to the gravity of each case. The ensuing climate of dissension and schism occasioned two of his most important works, the pastoral letters *Concerning the Lapsed* and *The Unity of the Church* (the latter being the first treatise ever on ecclesiology).

No sooner had some measure of peace been restored than a plague swept North Africa in 252. The death and devastation were blamed on Christianity's disrespect toward the Roman gods. So selflessly, so tirelessly did Cyprian go about his diocese, however, caring for the sick, regardless of their religion, organizing relief services, and consoling one and all, that even the pagans learned to admire him. Out of this episode came his *On Mortality.*

Next, there arose a controversy over the baptism conferred by heretics. Rome accepted it as valid; but Cyprian, faithful to the African position and to the teaching of Tertullian, was adamant on the need to rebaptize. This champion of unity repudiated the Roman tradition and even locked horns with Pope Stephen: in the very name of unity, Cyprian would recognize only one faith and one baptism—the one administered by the Church, the sole bride of Christ. The bitter dispute between these two good men (reminiscent of the earlier clash between Peter and Paul) was almost certain to end in tragedy.

But matters were never allowed to reach that stage. In August of 257, the Emperor Valerian promulgated an edict against the Christians. The result was a persecution in which Pope Stephen died for the faith and Cyprian was exiled to the town of Curubis for refusing to sacrifice to the gods. Recalled to Carthage the following year, he was summarily tried, sentenced and beheaded, just outside the city, on September 14, 258.

This model of bishops was the first African one to be martyred. Immediately after his death, he was venerated as a saint and for centuries honored as patron of Africa.

Cyprian the writer

As the second of the great African theologians, Cyprian might seem largely dependent on Tertullian, whom he read every day and always referred to as "the master." And, in fact, his admiration for Tertullian brought on a veritable inferiority complex, though there was no reason for it: what he lacked of Tertullian's boldness and fire and originality and provocativeness, he more than made up in wisdom, in prudence and moderation, in charity and urbanity. He is more readable than Tertullian, more classical and, at the same time, more profoundly influenced by the diction and imagery of Scripture.

Essentially a man of action, Cyprian was less interested in theological speculation than in the actual care of souls. Every item in his considerable literary output grew, as we saw in part, out of a concrete situation and served some practical purpose—being, so to speak, but a prolongation of his preaching.

The Lord's Prayer

Many of Cyprian's works incorporate the best of Tertullian's thinking, often in the form of quotations or allusions. Still, we must not imagine that Cyprian is a mere carbon copy of "the master," as some commentators seem to suggest. A case in point is the book which concerns us here, *The Lord's Prayer*. One popular guide to patrology disposes of it in two words: "like Tertullian's." A collection of the writings of the early Fathers says that Cyprian "imitates" the division used by Tertullian "in his book on prayer" and, "still treading in the footsteps of Tertullian . . . goes through [the prayer's] seven chief clauses." True, yet unfair in its implications.

The Lord's Prayer was composed toward the end of 251 or the beginning of 252, immediately after Cyprian had finished *The Unity of the Church* and when he was still intensely preoccupied with the ideal of unity. As a result, his commentary on the Our Father is filled with echoes of the earlier work. This alone would give it a unique ring.

For his outline he went to Tertullian's *De oratione*, from which he borrowed the threefold division—but little else. This latter fact is hardly surprising, since Tertullian's is a disciplinary work, whereas Cyprian's is a pastoral one; and since Tertullian's (as the title indicates) treats of prayer in general and almost incidentally comments on the Lord's Prayer, whereas Cyprian's (as, again, the title indicates) works quite the other way around. These differences allow Cyprian to probe far deeper and offer a more comprehensive and compelling treatment.

A hundred years later, when Hilary of Poitiers wrote his commentary on Matthew, he omitted the section containing the Lord's Prayer on the grounds that Cyprian had said all there was to say about it.

Cyprian and "the Jews"

The modern reader cannot but be disturbed by Cyprian's anti-Semitic—or, more properly, anti-Judaic—remarks, especially in Chapter 10 but also in 13 and 36. His harsh references to "the Jews" can be understood only in the historical and intellectual context that spawned them.

The moment the apostles began teaching and acting "in the name of Jesus Christ the Nazarene,"[3] tension arose between Synagogue and Church and intensified as each tried to explain its position. Because the proclamation of Christ's divinity seemed an assault on monotheism, and His Messiahship a blow at Israel's national pride, Synagogue leaders resorted to threats, arrests, exile, killings, a "great persecution,"[4] and multiform hostilities culminating in the excommunication of the "apostate and traitorous sect" in the year 80.

Meanwhile, the New Testament was being written. Human as well as divine, it reflects the ongoing situation and bears the marks of conflict; but, as Gregory Baum has shown in *Is the New Testament Anti-Semitic?*,[5] nowhere does it inculcate hatred or level unjust accusations and dire prophecies at the Jewish people. Jesus teaches, "Love your enemies; pray for your persecutors."[6] Paul insists that the Jews have not been cast off but are still "most dear," and that "God's gifts and call are irrevocable." Gladly would he be cursed "for the sake of my brothers."[7] Such was the Church's prime, authentic attitude toward the Jews: distinctness plus goodwill.

Unfortunately, another attitude prevailed when, around the year 100, the apologists emerged. Fearful of Jewish proselytism and of Judaizers within the Church, they forgot goodwill and pushed for distinctness unto total opposition. With the best of intentions, they searched the Scriptures for texts to prove that Israel had been unfaithful and so lost its providential mission; they applied John's *hoi Ioudaioi* to the whole Jewish people

---

[3] Acts 3:6.

[4] Acts 8:1.

[5] Glen Rock, N.J.: Paulist Press, 1965.

[6] Matthew 5:44.

[7] Romans 9:3, 11 and 11:28-29.

instead of some Jerusalem scribes, Pharisees and elders and the chief priests; and they misread events as signs of God's disapprobation. Justin was the first to say outright that the misfortunes of the Jewish nation were repayment for Christ's death—a theme that would be richly orchestrated in subsequent ages. Holy hate was, and would long be, the spirit of the times.

Into such an atmosphere Cyprian stepped when he entered the Church in 245. Though not surprising, neither is it edifying to see him join his predecessors and contemporaries in turning the Bible into a weapon against Judaism. Whence, his *Testimonia ad Quirinum*, two-thirds of which is an arsenal of Old Testament texts to be used in quashing the Jews; whence, also, the derogatory remarks here in *The Lord's Prayer.*

Blessedly, others were less defensive and heard the gospel message more consistently. Already in Cyprian's day, the *Didascalia*, while still holding "the Jews" responsible for Christ's death, called them "our brothers" and bade Christians fast for them during the Passover.[8] Later, the *Catechism of the Council of Trent* would declare that guilt for Christ's death "seems more enormous in us than in the Jews, since, says Paul, 'they would never have crucified Him had they known,' whereas we, professing to know Him, yet lay violent hands on Him."[9] But only with Vatican II would the Church's pristine position on the matter be stated unequivocally, inescapably.

What are we to do about Cyprian, then? Instead of discarding his slightly flawed masterpiece, let us apply to it the correctives indicated by the Council. When he says that calling God our *Father* "rebukes and condemns the Jews, who not only faithlessly spurned but cruelly executed the Christ" (Chapter 10),[10] and adds that they

---

[8] *Didascalia*, 21.

[9] Part I, Article 4.

[10] In the text proper, such *who*-clauses are rendered restrictively (that is, without commas)—a step in the right direction, but easily overlooked.

XIII

"have remained in darkness for having forsaken the light"
(Chapter 36), we must hear Vatican II asserting that
Christ's passion "cannot be blamed on all the Jews then
living, without distinction, nor upon the Jews of today,"
because these deeds were done only by "authorities of the
Jews and those who followed their lead." When he boasts
that God has begun to be our Father "but ceased to be
that of the Jews," since "there is no way a sinful nation
can be His children" (Chapter 10); when he urges us to
pray "lest we defect from the heavenly kingdom, like the
Jews, to whom it was promised first," and maintains that
"the Jews were formerly children of the kingdom as long
as they persevered in being children of God as well; but
after the name 'Father' disappeared from among them, so
did the kingdom" (Chapter 13), we must remember Vatican II's warning: "The Jews should not be represented as
repudiated or cursed by God, as if such views followed
from the holy Scriptures." That kind of thinking is "out of
harmony with the truth of the gospel and the spirit of
Christ." The Church "deplores" it, along with "the
hatred, persecutions and displays of anti-Semitism di-
rected against the Jews at any time and from any
source"—including the Fathers of the Church.[11]

Rather, with Cyprian himself in his wisest moments
(when not carried away by fear and oratorical fervor), we
can say the Lord's Prayer "for *all* . . . so that God's will
be done *for them*, too" (Chapter 17). And (since we are all
Semites spiritually) we can pray with Paul for our "brothers and kinsmen," who, as he says in the present tense,
"have the sonship and the glory and the covenant and the
legislation and the worship and the promises, who have
the patriarchs, and from whom comes Christ according to
the flesh."[12]

---

[11] All these correctives are from the Declaration on the Relationship of
the Church to Non-Christian Religions, Section 4, in *The Documents of
Vatican II*, edited by Walter M. Abbott, S.J. (New York: The America
Press, 1966), pp. 663-667.
[12] Romans 9:4-5.

A note on this translation

The title page bears the words "translated for meditation." That statement of fact and policy sums up my whole purpose while engaged in this most pleasant of tasks: to convey wholly and solely what Cyprian wrote, striving for accuracy rather than improvising (however modestly) on a given theme; and to keep the entire thing so simple that it would be directly conducive to prayer. There is no reason why exactitude and readability cannot go hand in hand—especially with the aid of various typographical devices.

For that reason, I have arranged the text in sense lines, with several degrees of indentation, a technique which startlingly X-rays an author's thought and allows the reader to follow easily, saying, "Here's the main idea, and that one is clearly subordinate. These phrases all bear the same relationship to this other point. Glad I didn't miss this parallelism or that antithesis. My, how that word hits you right between the eyes!"

It was also necessary to break up many of Cyprian's longer sentences whenever that could be done without weakening the thought or changing the emphasis. (The whole of Chapter 17, for example, was originally written as two sentences.) Though the rolling Ciceronian period delights the intellect, the terse apothegm jabs harder at the heart. Times and taste have changed, and Cyprian's message is far too vital to be kept tightly wrapped in its shroud.

The text handed down to us consists simply of brief chapters numbered from 1 to 36, without groupings or headings of any kind. To facilitate finding what one wants to meditate on at any particular time, I thought it useful to bring out (by means of Roman numerals and titles of my devisal) the implicit tripartite division which Cyprian borrowed from Tertullian; to group the thirty-six chapters (again, with my own titles) within that framework;

and, lastly, to divide those chapters into smaller thought units (by means of asterisks) when that seemed to clarify matters.

I have also added two kinds of footnotes: first, Scriptural references—mostly from the standard editions, but some from my mulling of the text; and, secondly, a few comments regarding the translation of a work or phrase, or remarks on some passage that could easily be taken amiss.

(Strictly speaking, all the additions mentioned in the two preceding paragraphs should be placed between brackets, but that would look clumsy and pedantic and soon prove annoying. The reader will understand, once and for all, that the content of the chapters and the numbering from 1 to 36 are from Cyprian, and that all else is meant to be editorial assistance.)

From the viewpoint of style, I have reduced many adjectives (as in *dilectissimi fratres*) from the superlative to the positive degree, since that is how the Romanized ear heard many of them anyway and they do tend to become a bit cloying and pompous in English. It also seemed advisable to pare down the synonymic couplings ("He prescribes and says," "Christ admonishes and warns," "we ask and pray"), a feature which adds to the luxuriance of Latin but does not transplant well.

More seriously from the standpoint of the scholar, I have occasionally altered pronouns for consistency. Ninety-five percent of the book is written in the first person plural, with occasional shifts to third singular and plural. Except when these shifts are required by the sense, I have tried to make the reading smoother by keeping to *we*.

Again, it frequently seemed desirable to spell out exactly what *hoc* or *quae* referred back to, particularly when they stood first in a new chapter.

The only glossing I have consciously permitted myself

is the introduction of two synonyms for *hallowed* in the second sentence of Chapter 12—something which appeared justified by the development in the rest of the chapter as well as by the quotation from 1 Corinthians; the insertion of *first* in the phrase "in his first letter," in the sixth sentence of Chapter 22 (since there are two other letters of John's); and, finally, the addition of *Eucharistic* in the third sentence of Chapter 31, since Cyprian is obviously referring to the Eucharistic prayer at Mass. If there are other instances of glossing, they are of the same kind as these.

*

It is my prayerful wish that the reader may draw even more light and strength than the translator from this little book.

E.B.

Part I:

Thoughts
on
prayer

1. Lessons from God

The gospel precepts,
               dear friends,
are, quite simply, lessons from God—
      foundations to build our hope on,
      supports to strengthen our faith,
      food to nourish our heart,
      rudders to guide our course,
      aids to reach salvation—
   which,
      by instructing
            our receptive, believers' minds
                here on earth,
      lead us to the kingdom of heaven.

God willed many other things to be said and heard
    through His servants, the prophets;
but how much greater are those His Son speaks—
    the things which the Word of God
       (who was in the prophets)
    proclaims with His own voice.

No longer does He bid us prepare the way
      for His coming,
but comes Himself in person,

opening and showing us the way;
so that we,
wandering once in the darkness of death,
mindless and blind,
but illumined now by the light of grace,
may walk the road to life
with the Lord as our leader and guide.

2. A format for prayer in spirit and in truth

Along with His other salutary admonitions
        and the divine precepts
    through which He counsels His people
        for their salvation,
He has also furnished a format for prayer.

He Himself has told us
    what to pray for.

With the same generosity
    that deigned to lavish all else on us,
He who gave us life
        has also shown us how to pray,
    so we may more readily be heard
    as we speak to the Father
        in the very words
            His Son has taught us.

*

Having already foretold
    that the hour was coming
        when true adorers would worship the Father

in spirit and in truth,[1]
He then fulfilled His promise.

As a result,
we who have received the Spirit and truth
through His sanctification
can also worship truly and spiritually
through His teaching.

For what prayer could be more spiritual
than the one given us by Christ,
who also sent us the Holy Spirit?

What prayer to the Father could be truer
than the one framed by the lips of the Son,
who is the Truth?

So that praying otherwise
would be not mere ignorance
but sin, too—
since He Himself declared,
"You reject the commandment of God,
to set up your own tradition."[2]

---

[1] John 4:23.
[2] Mark 7:8-9.

3. The very words of the Son

And so, dear friends, we should pray
    as the Lord our Teacher has taught us.

It is a loving and intimate prayer
    to entreat God in His own words,
    to gain His ear with the petition of Christ.

May the Father recognize His Son's words
    when we offer up our prayer.

May He who dwells in our inmost soul
    be present in our voice as well.

And since we have Him
    as advocate with the Father
        for our sins,
let us use the words of our advocate
    when we sinners seek forgiveness
        for those sins.

For if He promised,

"The Father will give you
　　anything you ask in my name,"[1]
how much surer we are to receive
　　what we ask in His name
　　　if we do so with His own prayer![2]

[1] John 16:23.
[2] See John 14:6.

4. Humble, heartfelt prayer

Still, when we pray,
    our words and petitions should be calm,
        filled with quiet modesty.

Let us remember
    we are standing in the sight of God,
        whom we must please
            both by our bearing
            and by our tone of voice.

For, though the impudent
    always clatter and clamor,
the reverent
    ought to present their requests humbly.

*

In His teaching, furthermore,
    the Lord bids us pray in secret—
        in hidden and secluded spots,
        in our very bedrooms—
because genuine faith should realize
    that God is present everywhere,
    that He hears and sees everyone,

and penetrates even remote, concealed places
>with the fulness of His majesty.

As it is written,
>"I am a God who is close at hand,
>>not some God afar off.
>Can anyone hide in a dark corner
>>without my seeing him?
>Do I not fill
>>both heaven and earth?"[1]

Or again,
>"The eyes of the Lord are everywhere,
>>observing the good and the wicked."[2]

*

And when we gather with our brothers
>to celebrate the sacred mysteries
>>with God's priest,
we must be reverent and reserved,
>not broadcasting our prayers
>>right and left
>>at the top of our lungs
>or flinging at God,
>>in a torrent of words,
>a petition that should commend itself to Him

---

[1] Jeremiah 23:23-24.
[2] Proverbs 15:3.

by its moderation.

For God listens,
    not to our voice,
    but to our heart.

He does not need to be prodded
      with shouts,
    since He sees our thoughts,
      as the Lord proved when He asked,
        "Why do you think evil in your hearts?"[3]

And elsewhere He stated:
    "All the churches shall know
      that I am he
        who searches minds and hearts."[4]

---

[3] Matthew 9:4.
[4] Revelation 2:23.

5. Not with her voice, but with her heart

In the first book of Samuel[1]
   we see this rule observed by Hannah,
      a type of the Church.

She entreated God,
   not with noisy pleas,
   but with silent humility
      in the very depths of her soul.

Her prayer was secret,
   but her faith was manifest.

She spoke,
   not with her voice,
   but with her heart—
      knowing that that is how God hears.

And she definitely obtained what she sought,
   because she asked it with faith.

Holy Scripture makes this clear when it says,

---

[1] Cyprian's reference is to 1 Kings.

"She prayed in her heart;
  though her lips moved,
    her voice could not be heard. . . .
And the Lord answered her prayer."[2]

Similarly, we read in the Psalms:
  "Speak in your heart,
  and in the privacy of your room repent."[3]

The Holy Spirit suggests the same thing,
    teaching us through Jeremiah:
  "Say in your hearts,
    'Master, it is you we must adore.'"[4]

---

[2] 1 Samuel 1:13, 20.
[3] Psalm 4:4.
[4] Baruch 6:5. Cyprian's quotation reads: "God ought to be adored by you in your heart."

6. Beating his breast and begging for mercy

As we worship,
  dear friends,
let us not forget, either,
 how the tax collector prayed
  with the Pharisee
   in the Temple—
 not arrogantly raising his eyes to heaven,
 not boldly waving his arms about,
 but beating his breast
 and, because of the sinfulness within,
 imploring the help of divine mercy.

Though the Pharisee was satisfied with himself,
 the other man,
   pleading this way,
 deserved all the more to be sanctified.

For he did not place his hope of salvation
  in the certainty of his own innocence
   (indeed, no one is innocent!),
 but, confessing his sins,
  prayed humbly;
and He who forgives the humble

heard him as he prayed.

This is what the Lord asserts in His gospel
     when He says,
  "Two men went up to the Temple to pray,
    one a Pharisee
  and the other a tax collector.
The Pharisee stood and prayed thus
       within himself:
  'O God, I thank you
    that I'm not like other men—
      dishonest,
      grasping
      and adulterous—
    especially not like this tax collector!
  I fast twice a week
    and pay tithes on all I possess.'
But the tax collector kept his distance
  and did not even raise his eyes heavenward
  but beat his breast and begged,
    'God, be merciful to me,
      a sinner.'
I assure you that he—
    not the Pharisee—
  went back home at rights with God.
For whoever exalts himself
  will be humbled,

and whoever humbles himself
will be exalted."[1]

---

[1] Luke 18:10-14.

Part II:

The
Lord's
Prayer

7. What to pray for

Dear friends,
>   now that we have learned
>>   from our sacred reading
>   how to approach prayer,
>   let us also learn
>>   from the Lord's teaching
>   what to pray for.

"Pray like this,"
>   He tells us:
>   "'Our Father,
>>   who are in heaven,
>   hallowed be your name;
>   your kingdom come;
>   your will be done on earth
>>   as it is in heaven.
>   Give us this day our daily bread;
>   and forgive us our debts
>>   as we forgive our debtors;
>   and do not allow us
>   to be led into temptation;[1]
>   but deliver us from evil.'"[2]

---

[1] Cyprian has *"et ne patiaris nos induci . . ."* instead of *"et ne nos inducas . . . ."*

[2] Matthew 6:9-13.

8. Praying for the whole People of God

Above all,
    the Teacher of Peace
      and Master of Unity
    did not want prayer to be viewed
      as something individualistic
             and self-centered.[1]

Accordingly,
    when we pray,
  we must not think only of ourselves.

For we do not say,
    "*My* Father, who are in heaven"
or
    "Give *me* this day *my* daily bread";
nor does each of us ask
    merely that his own debt be forgiven

---

[1] The usual rendering of *singillatim noluit et privatim precem fieri*, "did not want prayer to be offered individually and privately," contradicts Cyprian's teaching, the words of Jesus alluded to in Chapter 4: "The Lord bids us pray in secret—in hidden and secluded spots, in our very bedrooms," and the example of Jesus cited in Chapter 29: "He would go off into the wilderness and pray. . . . He went out into the hills and spent the whole night communing with God." Whether we pray alone or in a group, we should pray as members of the People of God for the whole People of God. In that sense, *all* our prayer is public and communal.

or seek security against temptation
      and deliverance from evil
  for himself alone.

For us,
  prayer is public
      and communal;
and when we pray,
  we do so,
    not for one,
    but for the whole People
  because we, the whole People, are one.

The God of Peace
  and Master of Harmony,
      who inculcated oneness,
wanted each one to pray for all,
  just as He Himself bore all in One.

*

The three young men
    bound in the blazing furnace
observed this law of prayer,
  blending their voices in praise,
      one in mind and heart.

The faithful witness of Scripture reports it
  and, by showing how they prayed,
  gives us an example
      to imitate in our own prayer
        so we may resemble them.

"Then all three,
  in unison,"
      says the Bible,
"intoned a hymn and blessed the Lord."[2]

They were speaking
          as with a single voice,
  though Christ had not yet taught them
      how to pray.

And therefore,
          as they prayed,
their words proved availing and effectual,
    because calm, simple, spiritual prayer
        merited God's grace.

*

So, too, we find the apostles and disciples
    praying together
        after the Lord's ascension.

---

[2] Daniel 3:51.

"All of them, with one accord,"
    says Scripture,
"joined in constant prayer
  together with the women
  and Mary, the mother of Jesus,
  and his brothers."[3]

They kept praying with one mind,
  demonstrating both their perseverance
       and their unity in prayer.

For God,
  who enables people of one mind
    to dwell peaceably under one roof,[4]
will admit into His heavenly, eternal home
  only those who are of one mind in prayer.

[3] Acts 1:14.
[4] Psalm 67:7 in the version Cyprian used.

9. *"Our Father, who are in heaven"*

Dear friends,
    what mysteries[1] we find
        in the Lord's Prayer!

How many
and how great they are—
        condensed in a few, brief words
        yet abounding in spiritual power,
      so that this digest of divine teaching
        omits absolutely nothing
        but includes all
            in our prayers and petitions!

*

"Pray like this,"
        says Christ:
  "'Our Father, who are in heaven.'"

As new persons,
      reborn
      and restored to our God by His grace,
we immediately say "Father,"

---

[1] Cyprian uses the word *sacramenta* ("signs").

because we have already begun
  to be His children.

"He came to his own,"
        writes John,
  "but they would not accept him.
To all who did receive him,
        however,
to all who believe in him,
  he .gave power
    to become children of God."[2]

*

From this moment on, then,
  we who have believed in Him
          and so been made children of God
  should start
    giving thanks
    and professing ourselves His children.

When declaring
  that our father is God-in-heaven,
we must also attest,
        in the very first words spoken
            after our new birth,
  that we have renounced
    our earthly, physical father

[2] John 1:11-12.

and started to have and acknowledge
    none but our heavenly one.[3]

It is written:
    "Those who told father and mother,
        'I do not know you,'
    and refused to recognize their children—
    they it is who have followed your law
        and kept your covenant."[4]

In His gospel,
    the Lord likewise forbids us
        to call any man on earth "father,"
            since we have one Father,
                who is in heaven.[5]

And to a disciple
    who had mentioned his dead father,
    He replied:
        "Let the dead bury their own dead";[6]

---

[3] Cyprian is not advocating disregard for parents but simply establishing a hierarchy of loyalties. "Anyone who prefers father or mother to me is not worthy of me; nor is anyone who prefers son or daughter worthy of me" (Matthew 10:37).

[4] Deuteronomy 33:9.

[5] Matthew 23:9.

[6] Matthew 8:22.

for the man had said
>his father was dead,
>whereas the Father of believers
>>is living!

10. Father of all believers

Nor is it enough,
dear friends,
to realize that we should call
Him who is in heaven
"Father."

We must add to the name
and say "*our* Father":
that is,
Father of those who believe,
Father of those who—
sanctified through Him
and restored by the birth
of spiritual grace—
have started to be children of God.

*

This name rebukes and condemns the Jews
who not only faithlessly spurned
but cruelly executed
the Christ
announced to them by the prophets
and sent to their nation first.

No longer may they call God
> their Father,
>> because the Lord confounds and refutes them,
>>> saying,
>>>> "Your father is the devil,
>>>>> and you choose to carry out his wishes.
>>>> He was a murderer from the start
>>>>> and never dwelt in the truth,
>>>>>> because there is no truth in him."[1]

And through the prophet Isaiah
> God cries out in anger:
>> "I have begotten and raised children,
>>> but they have despised me.
>> The ox knows its owner,
>>> and the donkey its master's manger;
>> yet Israel does not recognize me,
>>> my own people will not acknowledge me.
>> O sinful nation,
>>> people weighed down with guilt,
>>> breed of evildoers,
>>> lawless children,
>> you have turned your backs on the Lord
>>> and have provoked the Holy One of Israel!"[2]

They stand convicted

---

[1] John 8:44.
[2] Isaiah 1:2-4.

when we Christians,
    at prayer,
say "our Father,"
    since He has begun to be ours
    but ceased to be that of the Jews
      who have forsaken Him.

There is no way a sinful nation
    can be His children;
rather, that title is bestowed on those
    to whom remission of sins has been granted
      and eternal life promised.

The Lord Himself says:
    "Everyone who sins
      is the slave of sin.
    A slave has no permanent place
      in the household,
    but the son belongs there
      forever."[3]

---

[3] John 8:34-35.

11. To live like children of God

How kind the Lord is to us,
        how very merciful and good,
    to want us to pray
            in God's sight
    in such a way
        as to call Him our Father
        and be called His children in turn,
            even as Christ is His Son!

That is a title
    none of us would dare appropriate
            in prayer
    had He Himself not allowed us to.

*

And so, dear friends,
        since we call God our Father,
    let us remember
        to act like children of God,
            so that He may find pleasure
                in having us as His children,
            just as we do
                in having Him as our Father.

We must live like temples of God,
    so it may be evident
        that He dwells in us.

Let not our life-style clash
        with the Spirit;
instead,
    as we grow
        more spiritual and heavenly-minded,
may we think and do
        only spiritual and heavenly things.

For the Lord God Himself has said,
    "Those who honor me
      I will honor;
    and those who despise me
        shall themselves be despised."[1]

And the blessed Apostle, too,
        has stated in one of his letters:
    "You are not your own property,
      but were bought at a great price.
    So glorify and carry God about
        in your body."[2]

---

[1] 1 Samuel 2:30.
[2] 1 Corinthians 6:19-20.

12. *"Hallowed be your name"*

Then we say,
    "Hallowed be your name"—
  not wishing,
      for God,
    that He be hallowed by our prayers,
  but begging,
      from God,
    that His name be hallowed *in us.*

After all,
  by whom would God be hallowed,
    since He is the one who hallows,
          who sanctifies,
          who makes holy?

But because He Himself said,
    "Be holy,
      for I am holy,"[1]
we beg
  that we who have been sanctified
    through baptism
  may persevere in being
    what we have begun to be.

---

[1] Leviticus 20:7.

And this we implore daily
    because we need to be sanctified daily,
        so that we who sin continually
            may wash away our sins
                by continual sanctification.[2]

*

Now, this "sanctification,"
    which God graciously grants us,
is spelled out by the Apostle
        when he says:
    "No fornicator or idolater,
    no adulterer or effeminate or sodomite,
    no thief or extortioner,
    no drunkard or slanderer or swindler
        shall inherit the kingdom of God.
    Such you once were;
        but now you have been cleansed
                  and justified
                  and made holy
    in the name of our Lord Jesus Christ
    and the Spirit of our God."[3]

He says
    we have been *made holy*
        in the name of the Lord Jesus Christ
        and in the Spirit of our God!

---

[2] See Proverbs 24:16.
[3] 1 Corinthians 6:9-11.

*

What we are praying for
is that this holiness continue in us.

And because our Lord and Judge
warned the man
He had healed and filled with life
to sin no more,
lest he suffer something worse,[4]
we constantly ask this in our prayers.

This we entreat day and night:
that the sanctification and life-giving
received from God's grace
may be preserved in us
by His protection.

---

[4] John 5:14.

13. *"Your kingdom come"*

The prayer continues:
  "Your kingdom come."

We ask that the kingdom of God
    be made present *to us*,
just as we ask that His name
    be made holy *in us*.

For, when does God not reign?

Or,
    with Him,
how mark the beginning
        of what has always been
        and never ceases to be?

What we are praying for
    is the coming of *our* kingdom—
        the one promised us by God
        and gained by Christ's bloody passion—
    so that,
        having first served Him on earth,

we may then reign with Him as Lord,
　　as He guaranteed when He said:
　　　　"Come,

　　　　　　you whom my Father has blessed;
　　　　　　inherit the kingdom prepared for you
　　　　　　　from the beginning of the world."[1]

　　　　　　　　　　＊

It is also possible,
　　　　　dear friends,
for "the kingdom of God"
　　to be taken as Christ Himself—
　　　　Christ,
　　　　　　whose coming
　　　　　　　we desire day after day;
　　　　Christ,
　　　　　　whose coming
　　　　　　　we want manifested to us soon.

For, just as He Himself is the resurrection,
　　since we rise again in Him,
so, too, He can be called the kingdom of God,
　　since we are to reign in Him.

　　　　　　　　　　＊

Besides,

---

[1] Matthew 25:34.

we do well to seek the kingdom of God—
in other words, the heavenly kingdom—
for there is an earthly one also.

But if we have already renounced the world,
we are greater than both its honors
and its dominion;
and so, we who dedicate ourselves
to God and to Christ
desire, not the kingdom of earth,
but the kingdom of heaven.

*

There is need, however,
of constant prayer and petition,
lest we defect from the heavenly kingdom,
like the Jews
to whom it was promised first.

This the Lord makes unmistakably clear
by saying:
"Many will come from east and west
and recline at the banquet table
with Abraham and Isaac and Jacob
in the kingdom of heaven,
whereas those born to the kingdom
will be driven into the darkness outside—

there to wail and gnash their teeth."[2]

He shows that the Jews
    were formerly children of the kingdom
        as long as they persevered
           in being children of God
              as well;
    but after the name "Father" disappeared
            from among them,
    so did the kingdom.

And therefore we Christians,
    who have begun to call God our "Father"
        in prayer,
also plead that the kingdom of God
    may come to us.

---

[2] Matthew 8:11-12.

14. *"Your will be done on earth as it is in heaven"*

After that, we add:
    "Your will be done on earth
        as it is in heaven—
not so that *God* may do
        what He wants,
but that *we* may be able to do
        what He wants.

For who could hinder God
    from doing whatever He wishes?

But because the devil keeps us
    from always obeying God
        in thought and act,
we plead
    that God's will be done in us.

*

For this,
    we need His goodwill—
        in other words, His help and protection;
    for no one is strong enough

of himself,
but is secure
through divine grace and mercy.

Even the Lord,
in order to show the weakness
of the human nature He bore,
said,
"Father,
if it be possible,
let this cup pass from me";
and then,
to teach His disciples by example
that they should do,
not their own will,
but God's,
He added,
"Still, not as I want,
but as you want."[1]

*

Elsewhere He said:
"I have come down from heaven
to do,
not my own will,
but the will of him who sent me."[2]

---

[1] Matthew 26:39.
[2] John 6:38.

Now, if the Son obeyed
    and did His Father's will,
how much more should we servants obey
    and do our Master's will!

Hence, John in his first letter
       also instructs and urges us
          to do God's will:
"Do not love the world
    or the things in it.
If anyone does,
    he cannot love the Father.
For all there is in the world—
         fleshly lusts,
         covetous glances
         and earthly ambition—
comes, not from the Father,
    but from this itching world.
Yet, this world will pass away,
    together will all it craves for;
but whoever does God's will
    abides forever,
         just as God abides forever."[3]

We who desire to live eternally
    should do the will of God,
       who is eternal.

---

[3] 1 John 2:15-17.

15. Doing the Father's will

Now, the will of God is precisely
    what Christ both did and taught.

It entails
    being humble in our life-style,
                steadfast in our faith,
                modest in our words,
                just in our actions,
                merciful in our dealings,
                disciplined in our conduct,
                incapable of inflicting a wrong
                but able to bear one inflicted on us;
    keeping peace with our brothers;
    loving God with all our heart;
    cherishing Him as Father
                while fearing Him as God;
    putting absolutely nothing before Christ,
                since He put nothing before us;
    clinging tenaciously to His love;
    standing, brave and confident, by His cross;
    and,
        whenever His name
                    and honor are involved,
        displaying

in our speech
　　the constancy
　　　　to confess Him,
under torture
　　the courage
　　　　to fight for Him,
and in death
　　the patience
　　　　for which we shall be crowned.[1]

This is what it means
　　to want to be coheirs with Christ;
this is what it means
　　to carry out the commands of God;
this is what it means
　　to do the Father's will.

---

[1] These last twelve lines read like the scenario for Cyprian's own arrest, trials, banishment and martyrdom, which would take place some five or six years later. See "Acts of St. Cyprian" in *A Treasury of Early Christianity*, edited by Anne Fremantle (N.Y.: Mentor Books, 1953), pp. 197-200.

16. Man: both heaven and earth

Moreover,
    we ask that God's will be done
             in heaven
             and on earth,
    because both pertain
             to our total safety and salvation.

Indeed,
    holding our body from earth
             and our spirit from heaven,
we ourselves *are* earth and heaven
and pray
    that God's will be done in both—
             that is, in our body
                and in our spirit.

*

For there is a battle
    between flesh and spirit,
a daily warfare
    as they clash together.

Consequently, we fail to do
          the very things we wish,
   because the spirit seeks
     the heavenly and divine
while the flesh lusts after
    the earthly and profane.

And so we earnestly beg
   that harmony be achieved
        between these two forces,
    with God's help and assistance,
so that,
        as His will is being done
          in both the spirit
          and the flesh,
our soul
    (reborn through Him)
may be kept safe.

*

The Apostle Paul puts it plainly
       in these words of his:
  "The desires of the flesh
    run counter to the spirit's,
and the spirit's
    to those of the flesh;
for the two are opposed

to each other,
with the result that you do not do
the very things you want. . . .
Now, the deeds of the flesh are obvious:
adultery and fornication,

filth and indecency;
idolatry and occultism;
murder and hatred,

envy and jealousy,
anger and quarrels,
feuds and factions,
dissension and strife;
drunkenness and carousing;
and the like.
I warn you,

as I warned you before,
that those who do such things

will not inherit the kingdom of God.
But the fruit of the Spirit
is love and joy and peace,

patience, kindness,
fidelity, gentleness,
self-control and chastity."[1]

*

And, therefore, we pray daily—
or, rather, continually—
that God's will for us be done

---

[1] Galatians 5:17, 19-23.

both in heaven
and on earth,
because *this* is His will:
that earthly things
should give way to heavenly ones
and that spiritual and divine realities
should prevail.

17. Salt to save the whole earth

Dear friends,
    this petition can be interpreted
            still another way.

Since the Lord orders and warns us
        to love our enemies
        and pray for our very persecutors,[1]
we are being urged to intercede
    for those also
            who are still "of earth"
            and have not yet started
                to be heavenly-minded,
        so that God's will *for them* be done, too—
            that will which Christ accomplished
                by saving and renewing mankind.

*

He no longer calls His followers "earth,"
    but "salt of the earth."

And the Apostle describes the first man
    as being "from the dust of the earth,"

---

[1] See Matthew 5:44.

but the second
    as being "from heaven."[2]

It is only right, then,
    that we,
        who ought to resemble God our Father
            (who makes His sun rise
                on good and bad alike
            and lets His rain fall
                on righteous and unrighteous),
    should pray,
        as Christ reminds us,
        for the salvation of *all*.

And this will be the result
        of our intercession:
just as God's will has been done "in heaven"
        (that is, in us by our faith)
    and we have become heavenly-minded,
so, too, shall His will be done "on earth"
        (that is, in those who refuse to believe)
    and they who are still "of earth"
        from their first birth
    will start to be heavenly-minded
        when born of water and the Spirit.

---

[2] 1 Corinthians 15:47.

18. *"Give us this day our daily bread"*

We then go on to say:
"Give us this day our daily bread."

These words may be taken
either spiritually
or literally,
because, in the divine plan,
both readings are helpful for salvation.

*

The bread of life is Christ;
now, this is not everyone's bread,
but it *is ours*.

We say *"our* Father"
because He is the Father of those
who know and believe in Him;
so, too, we call this *"our* bread"
because Christ is the bread of those
who partake of[1] His body.

---

[1] This verb (*contingunt*) can also mean "are in union with"—and well we know Cyprian's constant preoccupation with the unity of the Church, the Mystical Body. In the present context, however, it seems to have its more usual meaning of "taking" communion, "reaching out to grasp" our food, the body of Christ, like the synonym (*attingunt*) four sentences below.

*

And we ask
　　that this bread be given us daily,
　lest we,
　　who live in Christ
　　and receive the Eucharist every day
　　　　as the food of salvation,
　be separated from His body
　　by some grave sin
　　　　that keeps us from communion
　　　　and so deprives us of our heavenly bread.

*

He Himself declares:
　"I am the bread of life
　　which has come down from heaven.
　If anyone eats my bread,
　　he will live forever.
　And the bread I shall give
　　is my flesh—
　　　　for the life of the world."[2]

He is telling us
　that anyone who eats His bread
　　will live forever.

Clearly, then,
> those who rightfully receive the Eucharist
> > and partake of Christ's body
>
> possess life.

*

And, just as clearly,
> we have reason to fear and pray
> > lest someone
> > > who is separated from Christ's body
> > > > by being kept from communion
> > be also cut off from salvation.

This He warned us of
> > when He said:
> > "Unless you eat the flesh of the Son of Man
> > > and drink His blood,
> > you will not have life in you."[3]

And so we aks
> for our bread—
> > that is, Christ—
> to be given us every day,
> so that we
> > who abide and live and Him
> may not drift away

---

[3] John 6:53.

from His body
and the sanctification it brings.

19. Only what we need, only for today

On the other hand,
    this petition can also mean
  that we
      who have renounced the world
      and cast aside its riches and glamour,
          trusting in grace from above,
    ought to request for ourselves
      only the food we really need
          in order to live.

As the Lord teaches,
    "Whoever does not give up all he has
        cannot be my disciple."[1]

When we have started
            to be followers of Christ
    and have renounced everything,
        as our Master demands,
  we should ask for *this* day's food
  and not allow our anxious prayer
      to race too far ahead.

[1] Luke 14:33.

For, again, the Lord cautions us:
"Do not worry about tomorrow;
tomorrow will take care of itself.
Each day has troubles enough of its own."[2]

Rightly, then, do Christ's followers
(forbidden to think of the morrow)
ask sustenance for themselves
one day at a time,
because it is inconsistent
and self-contradictory
to seek to live in this world
a long time
and yet pray for God's kingdom to come
swiftly.

*

The blessed Apostle, also, admonishes us
in the same vein,
grounding and reinforcing
our solid hope and faith:
"We brought nothing into this world,
nor can we take anything out of it;
but as long as we have food and clothing,
let us rest content.
People who long to be rich
fall into temptation

---

[2] Matthew 6:34.

and snares
and many harmful desires
that plunge them into ruin and perdition:
For the love of money
is the root of all evils;
and, in their craving for it,
some have strayed from the faith
and impaled themselves on many griefs."[3]

---

[3] 1 Timothy 6:7-10.

20. Gathering treasure in heaven

The Apostle explains
  that wealth is not only deserving of scorn
      but full of danger besides;
  that it holds the root of seductive evils,
    which beguile the blindness
      of the human mind
        with subtle lies.

Which is why God rebukes the stupid rich man
  who is all taken up
    with his earthly goods
  and boasts
    of his overflow bumper crops.

"You fool,"
    says God,
  "this very night
you must render up your soul.
And everything you have hoarded—
  whose will it be then?"[1]

The idiot was rejoicing in his harvest,

---

[1] Luke 12:20.

though he would die that same night;
he was thinking of heaped-up provisions,
though his life was already running out.

*

On the other hand, however,
    the Lord teaches
that we become perfect and complete
    when,
        selling all our possessions
        and giving the proceeds to the poor,[2]
    we gather treasure for ourselves
                in heaven.

He says
    we can follow Him
    and imitate the glory of His passion
        when,
            free of entanglement
                    in personal property,
            unfettered,
            unencumbered
            and ready for action,
        we ourselves accompany the possessions
            which we have sent on ahead
                to the Lord.

---

[2] Precisely what Cyprian did on becoming a Christian in 245.

So each of us may be able
      to prepare himself for that,
let us learn to pray in this spirit
and,
    from the wording of the petition,
know what sort of people we should be.

21. The kingdom first, and all the rest besides

For daily bread cannot be lacking
      to the righteous,
  since Scripture says:
     "The Lord will not torment
       the holy with hunger,"[1]
  and again:
     "I was young once,
         and now I am old;
     but never have I seen
      a good man forsaken
      or his children begging bread."[2]

And the Lord makes the same promise:
    "Do not worry or keep asking,
      'What are we to eat?
      What are we to drink?
      What are we to wear?'
    Unbelievers fret over such things.
    But, as for you,
      your heavenly Father knows
        you need all this.
    Set your hearts
      on the kingdom of God

---

[1] Proverbs 10:3.
[2] Psalm 37:25.

and his righteousness,
    first and foremost,
and all the rest will be given you
    as well."[3]

To those who yearn
    for God's kingdom and righteousness,
He pledges
    that all else will be added besides.

For, since everything is God's,
    nothing will fail those who possess God
        unless they themselves fail *Him*.

                *

Thus heaven provided food for Daniel,
    who had been thrown into a lion's den
        by order of the king;
and the man of God was fed there,
    among the voracious beasts
        that spared him.

Thus Elijah was nourished
    by ministering ravens
        when he fled into the wilderness,

---

[3] Matthew 6:31-33.

maintained
    by birds that brought him food
      when he was persecuted.

Oh, the revolting cruelty
      of human malice:
    that men should scheme and rage
      while savage beasts draw back
      and birds dispense food!

22. *"And forgive us our debts as we forgive our debtors"*

Next, we consider our sins,
            praying,
        "And forgive us our debts
            as we forgive our debtors."

Having sought food for subsistence,
    we now seek the remission of our sins,
        so that we
                who are fed by God
        may live in God
        and may provide
                not just for this present, passing life
                but also for eternal life,
                    into which we can enter
                        if our sins are forgiven.

These sins are what the Lord calls "debts,"
        as when He says in His gospel:
    "I canceled your entire debt
        because you begged me to."[1]

*

---

[1] Matthew 18:32.

How necessary it is,
      how farsighted and beneficial,
for us to be reminded
   that we are sinners
      obliged to plead for forgiveness,
        with the result that,
            as we implore God's pardon,
        our soul is kept conscious of its guilt!

Lest any of us grow smug
      about our supposed innocence
  and be doubly damned
      for extolling ourselves,
this command to *pray daily*
  because of our sins
tells us that we *sin daily.*

John warns us of this
      in his first letter:
  "If we claim to be sinless,
    we are deluding ouselves
    and living in falsehood.
  But if we admit our sins,
    then the Lord,
      who is faithful and just,
    will forgive them."[2]

---

[2] 1 John 1:8-9.

*

Two things are being stated here:
    that we should pray
        on account of our trespasses,
    and that we obtain pardon
        when we do.

Therefore John says
    that the Lord keeps His word
    and does indeed remit sin,
        because He who taught us to pray
            about our debts and sins
        promised to show us
            fatherly mercy and forgiveness.

23. Measured with our own yardstick

To the fulfilling of that promise
    Christ clearly attached
        a hard-and-fast condition,
                binding us by contractual agreement:
we are to ask
    that our debts be forgiven us
        to the extent we forgive our debtors—
aware that we cannot obtain the pardon
        we seek for our offenses
    unless we have granted the same pardon
        to those who offend against us.

Therefore He says elsewhere:
"The very yardstick you apply to others
    will be applied to you."[1]

Thus, the servant
    whose master had canceled his entire debt
was thrown back into prison
    for refusing to let off a fellow-servant;
because he would not extend the same leniency
        to another,
    he lost it for himself.

---

[1] Matthew 7:2.

*

Christ puts this idea still more forcefully
in His teaching
and roundly rebukes such conduct:
"When you stand up to pray,"
He says,
"forgive whatever you have against anyone,
so your heavenly Father may forgive you
your failings, too.
But if you do not,
neither will he forgive you."[2]

We will have no excuse
on judgment day,
when we are judged
according to our own decrees:
what we have done to others
will now be done to us.

*

God bids us be peace-making,
of one mind and heart,
in His home.[3]

Having made us what we are

---

[2] Mark 11:25.
[3] See Psalm 68:6.

by our second birth,
He wants us to continue being
these reborn creatures,
so that we who have started
to be God's children
may dwell in God's peace
and we who have but one Spirit
may also have one mind and heart.

Therefore God rejects our sacrifice
when we are at odds with our brothers
and orders us to leave the altar
and first be reconciled with them,
so He may be appeased by prayers
from hearts that are at peace.

The greatest sacrifice we can offer God
is our peacefulness,
our brotherly accord—
a people made one
in the oneness of Father,
Son
and Holy Spirit.

24. The heart, not the gift

Even in the sacrifices
    Cain and Abel offered long ago,
God looked,
        not at their gifts,
        but at their hearts,
   and the gift He accepted
   came from the heart that pleased Him.

Peace-loving, righteous and innocent
        as he sacrificed to God,
Abel teaches the rest of us,
     when presenting our gift at the altar,
   to come,
       as he did,
  in the fear of God,
  in simplicity of heart,
  in the holiness of the law,
  in peace and harmony.

Since he offered sacrifice so perfectly,
   it was only fitting
      that he himself later became a sacrifice
        to God;

and so,
  being the first example of martyrdom,
this man,
    who possessed both the Lord's holiness
            and peace,
inaugurated the Lord's passion
  in the glory of his own blood.

Such, then, are those
  whom the Lord crowns;
such are those
  who will sit with Him in judgment
      on the last day.[1]

*

On the other hand
        (as the blessed Apostle
          and Holy Scripture testify),
even if a quarrelsome, dissident person,
        ever wrangling with his brothers,
were put to death for the sake of Christ,
  he could not shrug off the crime
    of internal disunion.

For it is written:
  "Anyone who hates his brother
    is a murderer."[2]

---

[1] See Matthew 19:28, 1 Corinthians 6:2-3, and Jude 1:15.
[2] 1 John 3:15.

Now, no murderer
    enters into the kingdom of heaven
    and lives with God;
no one who preferred to imitate Judas
        rather than Christ
    can then be with Christ.

What a sin that must be
    if it cannot be washed away
        by the baptism of blood!

What a crime
    if it cannot be expiated
        by martyrdom!

25. *"And do not allow us to be led into temptation"*

Of necessity also
    the Lord has us ask,
        "And do not allow us
            to be led into temptation."

In this part of the prayer,
    He shows
        that the enemy is powerless against us
           without God's prior permission.

During temptation, consequently,
    all our fear and devotion and attention
        should be focused on God,
      since evil has only such force
           as He Himself grants it.[1]

Scripture proves this when it says:
    "Nebuchadnezzar,
        king of Babylon,
    came to Jerusalem
      and besieged it;
    and the Lord gave Jehoiakim,

---

[1] See 1 Corinthians 10:13.

> king of Judah,
> into his hands."[2]

*

Moreover,
> evil is given power over us
>> according to our sins.

As Isaiah writes,
> "Who gave Jacob up to the looters,
>> and Israel to the spoilers?
> It was the Lord,
>>> against whom we sinned,
>>> in whose ways we would not walk,
>>> and whose law we refused to obey.
> So he unleashed the fury of his anger
>>> against us."[3]

And again,
> when Solomon sinned
> and strayed from the precepts and paths
>> of the Lord,
it was recorded:
> "The Lord stirred up Satan
>> against Solomon himself."[4]

---

[2] Daniel 1:1; also 2 Kings 24:11-16.
[3] Isaiah 42:24-25.
[4] 1 Kings 11:14 (so Cyprian's text).

26. Lest we forget our frailty

Now, this power is granted in two ways:
    either for punishment
        when we fail in our duty
    or for glory
        when we are tried and found true.

This happened to Job,
        as God plainly states:
    "See here!
        Everything he has
            I place under your control,
        but do not lay a finger
            on Job himself."[1]

And in His gospel the Lord says
        at the time of His passion:
    "You would have no power over me
        unless it were given you from above."[2]

*

Furthermore,
    having to ask

---

[1] Job 1:12.
[2] John 19:11.

not to fall into temptation
reminds us
how weak and insecure we are.

It keeps us
from strutting about
with our nose in the air,
from arrogantly claiming to be
something we are not,
from considering as our own
the glory of professing our faith
or suffering for it.

Which is why the Lord Himself,
inculcating humility,
told us,
"Be alert and pray
not to fall into temptation;
for the spirit is willing,
but the flesh is weak."[3]

If we start
by humbly admitting our need
and ascribing all good to God,
whatever we implore,

---

[3] Matthew 26:41.

through fear of Him
and for His honor,
He will grant us
in His loving-kindness.

27. *"But deliver us from evil"*

After all these requests,
    the prayer ends with a brief clause
        that pithily sums up
            all our desires and petitions.

We conclude by saying,
    "But deliver us from evil."

This covers everything harmful
    which the enemy tries against us
            in this world,
    but from which we can find
            sure and powerful protection
        if God delivers us
        and grants us His help,
            as we implore.

When we say,
    "Deliver us from evil,"
there remains nothing further to ask for.

Once we have sought and obtained

God's protection
from evil,
we stand safe and secure
against all the machinations
of the devil and the world.

For what is there to fear
in this life
when,
in this life,
our guardian is God?

Part III:

Further
thoughts
on prayer

28. So much in so few words

Is it any wonder,
　　　dear friends,
　　that God gave us this sort of prayer?

After all,
　　　in His teaching
He had a way of capsulizing
　　our every prayer
　　　in a single saving sentence.

This had already been foretold
　　　by the prophet Isaiah
when,
　　　　inspired by the Holy Spirit,
he spoke of God's majesty
　　　　　and loving-kindness
as "carrying out his decree
and bringing it to swift fulfillment
　　in accord with justice,
　　since God will give short shrift
　　　to the whole land."[1]

For when the Word of God,

---

[1] Isaiah 10:22-23, where it is being said that there is dire punishment in store for Judah and that only a remnant of Israel will return from exile.

our Lord Jesus Christ,
came among us all,
He gathered together
men and women,
young and old,
learned and unlearned,
and taught them His saving doctrine.

Then He would draw up a complete summary
of that doctrine,
so that His followers' memory
would not be taxed
with His heavenly teaching
but might quickly absorb
the basics of a simple faith.

*

Thus,
when He taught the meaning of eternal life,
He outlined its mystery
with powerful, divine terseness,
saying,
"This is eternal life:
to know you,
the only true God,
and Jesus Christ,
whom you have sent."[2]

---

[2] John 17:3.

Similarly,
    when citing the first and greatest commandment
        in the Law and the Prophets,
He announced:
    "Hear this, Israel:
        'The Lord your God
            is the only Lord,
      and you shall love the Lord your God
            with all your heart
            and all your soul
            and all your might.'
    That is the first commandment.
    And the second resembles it:
        'You shall love your neighbor
            as yourself.'
    On these two commandments
        hinge the whole Law and the Prophets."[3]

Another time, He declared:
    "Treat others
        as you want them to treat you.
    That is the meaning
        of the Law and the Prophets."[4]

---

[3] Mark 12:29-31, conflated with Matthew 22:37-40.
[4] Matthew 7:12.

29. The example of Christ

It was not only by His words
       but by His actions also
    that the Lord taught us
       how to pray.

He Himself prayed
       frequently and earnestly
and,
       by the testimony of His example,
showed us what we should do.

As is recorded,
    "He would go off
          into the wilderness
    and pray."[1]

And again:
    "He went out
       into the hills
          to pray
    and spent the whole night
       communing with God."[2]

---

[1] Luke 5:16.
[2] Luke 6:12.

*

Now,

    if He who was sinless prayed,
how much more should we sinners do so!

And if He kept watch
    the whole night through,
  praying constantly
    with uninterrupted petitions,
how much more should we stay awake
      at night
    in continuous prayer![3]

---

[3] This idea, repeated in Chapter 35 and three more times in Chapter 36, is no rhetorical exaggeration but a profound conviction of Cyprian's. If it sounded impractical—no: downright impossible—in his day, it sounds even more so now, in the "jet age," this "age of anxiety," of deadlines, committees, moonlighting and multiform pressures, when so many of us suffer from nervous exhaustion and cannot afford to curtail our sleep. Cyprian was far too sensible to suggest that we do much of that. Instead, he was thinking along the same lines as St. Paul: "Whether you eat or drink—whatever you do—do all for the glory of God" (1 Corinthians 10:31). What theologians call a "virtual intention" is something very real. The morning offering we say daily covers all twenty-four hours of the day—and, indeed, every moment of our entire life if we are praying sincerely. And there is such a thing as a "night offering"—willing again that our every breath and our every heartbeat during the night be so many acts of loving adoration. Thus we do what Cyprian himself urges in Chapter 31: we *"watch with our heart* even when our eyes are closed in sleep." That is what he meant by "staying awake at night in continuous prayer"; that enables us truly to say, like the bride in the Song of Songs, "I sleep, but my heart is awake."

30. Redeemed and prayed for

Moreover,
    the Lord prayed and pleaded,
      not for Himself
          (why would He
            who was innocent
            pray on His own behalf?),
    but because of our sins.

That is what He asserted
      when He said to Peter,
    "Listen!
    Satan has asked to sift all of you
      like wheat.
    But I have prayed for you,
      Simon,
      so your faith may not fail."[1]

And afterwards He prayed to the Father
      for all of us,
        saying,
    "Not only for these
      do I pray,
    but also for those

---

[1] Luke 22:31.

who will come to believe in me
through their word.
May they all be one!
Just as you are in me
and I am in you,
Father,
so may they be one in us!"[2]

*

In the interest of our salvation,
the Lord's kindness and compassion
are both boundless—
so that,
not content with redeeming us
by His blood,
He prayed for us besides.

*

And see what He asked for:
that,
just as Father and Son are one,
we, too, might abide in that oneness.

From this we can also understand
how seriously we sin
when we shatter unity and peace,

---

[2] John 17:20-21.

since the very Lord begged for these things.

He wanted His people to be saved
                    and live in peace,
     for He knew that discord cannot enter
        into the kingdom of God.

31. With wholehearted attention

When we stand to pray,
                    dear friends,
    we should pay wholehearted attention
        to what we are saying.

Let all fleshly,
            worldly thoughts vanish,
and our mind dwell solely
        on what it seeks.

Thus, the celebrant,
        introducing the Eucharistic prayer,
prepares our mind by saying,
        "Lift up your hearts";
and when we answer,
        "We lift them up to the Lord,"
we are cautioned
        to think of nothing
                but the Lord.

*

Our heart must be closed
            against the adversary,

and lie open
>to God alone,
>not allowing His enemy to draw near
>>at the time of prayer.

For he frequently creeps up on us,
>>worms his way in
>>and subtly sidetracks our prayer
>>>away from God,
>so that our lips may be saying
>>one thing
>but our hearts are thinking
>>of another—
>when, in fact, it is,
>>not the sound of our voice,
>>but our soul and our mind
>that should be praying to God
>>with purity of intention.

*

How careless
>to be swept away and captivated
>>by foolish, profane thoughts
>>>when praying to the Lord!

As if anything could be more important
>than the fact of speaking to God!

How can we ask Him to listen to us
  if we do not listen to ourselves?

How expect Him to be mindful of us
    as we pray
  if we are not mindful of ourselves?

     *

That is being totally off guard
  in the face of the enemy;
that is offending the majesty of God
    by our negligence
  in the very act of praying to Him;
that is holding our eyes open
  but letting our heart doze off.

We Christians, on the contrary,
  should watch with our heart
    even when our eyes are closed in sleep;
as the Song of Songs says of the Church,
  "I sleep,
    but my heart is awake."[1]

Therefore the Apostle warns us
    earnestly and wisely:
  "Persevere in prayer

---

[1] Song of Songs 5:2.

and be watchful in it"[2]—
meaning that,
when God sees
we are attentive at prayer,
we can obtain
what we ask of Him.

[2] Colossians 4:2.

32. Prayer backed by good works

But when we pray,
> we must not approach God
>> with bare, barren requests.

Petition is ineffectual
> when we offer Him sterile prayers.

For if every tree
> that bears no fruit
is cut down
and thrown on the fire,[1]
surely, words that bear no fruit
> cannot deserve God's favor,
>> because they remain unproductive.

Hence, Holy Scripture tells us:
> "Prayer is good
>> when joined with fasting
>>> and alms."[2]

The God who will reward us

---

[1] See Matthew 7:19.
[2] Tobit 12:8.

for our good deeds and alms
on judgment day,
even in this life listens kindly
to prayer backed by works.

*

Thus, Cornelius,
the Roman centurion,
deserved to be heard
when he prayed.

He was a man
who gave generously
to the Jewish people
and prayed constantly
to God.

As he was praying
around three o'clock one afternoon,
an angel appeared to him,
bore testimony to his deeds
and said,
"Cornelius,
your prayers and alms have risen
as a memorial
in the sight of God."[3]

---

[3] Acts 10:3-4.

33. Good works, a fragrant sacrifice to God

Swiftly do our prayers rise
        to God
   when the merit of our labor
     urges them upon Him.

*

Thus, the angel Raphael,
   a witness to Tobit's constant prayers
        and contant good works,
told him:
   "It is well to publish and proclaim
        God's deeds. . . .
   When you and Sarah prayed,
     I brought the remembrance of your prayers
       into his glorious presence;
   each time you buried the dead directly,
     I was with you;
   the day you unhesitatingly rose from table,
        leaving your meal untouched,
   and went out and hid that corpse,
     I had been sent to test you;
   and once again God has sent me—
     this time to cure you
        and your daughter-in-law, Sarah.

I am Raphael,
>one of the seven holy angels
>>who stand in God's glorious presence
>>to serve him."[1]

*

Through Isaiah also,
>the Lord warns us
>and teaches the same thing:
"Burst every bond of injustice,
>untie the knots of hard bargains,
let the oppressed enjoy peace,
>and void all unjust contracts.
Break your bread with the hungry,
>and take the homeless poor into your home;
clothe those who have nothing on their back,
>and do not ignore your own relatives.
Then your light will shine like the dawn,
>and your cure will come quickly;[2]
your righteousness will precede you,
>and the glory of God will surround you.
Then you will call out,
>and God will answer you;
while you are still speaking,
>he will say, 'Here I am!'"[3]

---

[1] Tobit 12:7, 12-15.

[2] The version Cyprian used was mistranslated and came out reading: "Your garments will spring forth speedily." God is saying, "Do the kind of penance I require, and your wounds will soon be healed."

[3] Isaiah 58:6-9.

He assures us
    that He is present,
    that He hears and protects
        those who cast the bonds of injustice
            out of their heart
        and give alms
            to the members of God's family
              according to His commands;
because,
    in hearing
        what God wants done,
they also deserve
    that He hear them.

*

When the brothers helped him
        in time of need,
the blessed Apostle Paul said
    that the good works people do
        are sacrifices offered to God.

"I have all I need,"
    he wrote,
"now that Epaphroditus has brought
    the gifts you sent—
        a sweet fragrance,
        a sacrifice

acceptable and pleasing to God."[4]

For, when we have pity on the poor,
    we are lending to God at interest;
and when we give to the lowly,
    we are giving to God:
in a spiritual sense,
    we are sacrificing
        a sweet fragrance to Him.

---

[4] Philippians 4:18.

34. Special times for prayer

We notice
    that the three young men with Daniel,
        strong in faith
        and victorious in captivity,
    prayed at the third, sixth and ninth hours,[1]
        as a symbol,[2] so to speak, of the Trinity,
        which would be revealed
           at a later time.

Here is what I mean:
    as the first hour moves toward the third,
        it shows the full number of the Trinity;
    as the fourth moves toward the sixth,
        it proclaims a second Trinity;
    and when,
           starting from the seventh,
    the ninth is completed,
        the perfect Trinity is numbered
           every three hours.

*

Having long ago determined
    these intervals of hours

---

[1] That is, at 9:00 A.M., 12:00 noon and 3:00 P.M.
[2] Cyprian uses the word *sacrament* ("sign").

and given them a spiritual meaning,
    the righteous observed them
        as set and proper times for prayer.

Later, it became evident
    that this schedule of worshiping God
        had prefigured things to come.

*

For the Holy Spirit descended
    upon the disciples
        at the third hour,
    fulfilling the grace
    of the Lord's promise.

Likewise,
    at the sixth hour,
Peter went up to the roof terrace,
    where both a sign
        and a voice from God
    instructed him
        to admit everyone
          to the grace of salvation,
        despite his previous doubts
          about baptizing the Gentiles.

And, finally, the Lord,
    crucified from the sixth hour
      to the ninth,
washed our sins away
    in His blood
and then completed the victory
    by His passion,
  so that He might be able
    to redeem us
    and give us life.

35. Morning and evening—and always

But for us today,
             dear friends,
          besides the hours for praying
             observed of old,[1]
both the times and the symbols of prayer
     have increased in number.

                              *

For instance,
     we should pray early, too,
          so that the Lord's resurrection
             may be celebrated
                by morning prayer.

The Holy Spirit once indicated this
          when He said in the Psalms:
     "Listen to the sound of my cry,
          O my King and my God;
             for to you, O Lord, will I pray.
     In the morning you shall hear my voice;
          I will stand before you early

---

[1] As we read in the Acts of the Apostles, for example. See 2:1-15 for the third hour, 10:9 for the sixth, and 3:1 for the ninth. For midnight, see 16:25. For constant prayer, see 1:14 and 2:42-47, among other texts.

and contemplate you."[2]

And again the Lord says
    through the prophet:
 "They will seek me at daybreak,
   saying,
  'Let us go and return
    to the Lord our God.'"[3]

       *

Similarly,
 when the sun sets
 and day draws to a close,
we must of necessity pray again.

For Christ is the true sun
    and the true day;
and,
 as this world's sun and day decline
 and we beg
   for light to return anew,
we pray for the coming of Christ
 to bring us the grace of everlasting light.

       *

---

[2] Psalm 5:2-3. Cyprian does not quote the first line but starts in mid-sentence, at "O my King."

[3] Hosea 6:1.

Furthermore,
> the Holy Spirit,
>> in the Psalms,
>> declares that Christ is called "the day."

He says:
> "The stone the builders rejected
>> has become the cornerstone.
> This is the Lord's doing,
>> and it is wonderful in our sight.
> This is the day the Lord has made:
>> let us exult and rejoice in it."[4]

The prophet Malachi also testifies
> that Christ is called "the sun."

"Upon you
>> who revere the name of the Lord,"
>> he says,
"the sun of righteousness shall arise,
> and in his rays there is healing."[5]

*

But if,
> according to Holy Scripture,

---

[4] Psalm 118:22-24. Cyprian's text has: "Let us *walk* and rejoice in it."
[5] Malachi 4:2. *Rays*: literally, *wings*.

Christ is the true sun
and the true day,
there is no time
when Christians should not be adoring God
often and always.

Consequently, we who are in Christ
(that is, in the true sun
and the true day)
should pursue our prayers and petitions
all through the day;
and when,
in nature's cycle,
night comes stealing over us again,
darkness must not spell the end of prayer
because,
for the children of light,
even nighttime is day.[6]

For when are we deprived of light
if we have light in our heart?

Or when is it not sunny daytime
if our sun and our day is Christ?

---

[6] See Psalm 139-12, where the singer says to God: "Even the darkness is not dark to you; no, the night is as bright as day, since, for you, darkness is like light itself."

36. Unceasing prayer, preview of eternity

Therefore,
> let us
>> who are in Christ
>>> (that is, always in the light)
>> not stop praying—
>>> not even during the night.

Thus, the widow Anna,
> ever praying and watching
>> without intermission,
continued to deserve God's blessings.

As the gospel says of her,
> "She never left the Temple,
>> but served night and day
>>> with fasting and prayer."[1]

        *

The pagans,
> who are not yet enlightened,
should ponder this.

---

[1] Luke 2:37.

So should the Jews
　　　who have remained in darkness
　　　　　for having forsaken the light.

　　　　　　　*

As for us,
　　　who are always in the light of the Lord,
　　　　　dear friends,
　　　and who remember and hold fast
　　　　　to what we have begun to be
　　　　　　by the gift of grace,
we ought to consider night as day.

Let us believe
　　　that we always walk in the light,[2]
and not be hindered
　　　by the darkness we have escaped.[3]

There should be no letup in prayer
　　　　　during the night hours,
no idle, cowardly waste of prayer-time.

Since we have been spiritually re-created
　　　　　　　and reborn
　　　　　through the mercy of God,

---

[2] See John 8:12 and 1 John 1:7.
[3] See Colossians 1:13.

let us imitate
what we shall one day be.

Since we are to enjoy unending day
in the kingdom-without-night,
let us, even now, watch through the night
as though it were day.

Since we are to pray
and give thanks to God
eternally,
let us, even here, never cease
to pray and give Him thanks.